Abbie's God Book

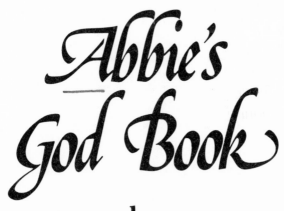

*Abbie's
God Book*

by
ISABELLE HOLLAND

Drawings by James McLaughlin

The Westminster Press
Philadelphia

Book Design by Alice Derr

First edition

Published by The Westminster Press ®
Philadelphia, Pennsylvania

PRINTED IN THE UNITED STATES OF AMERICA
9 8 7 6 5 4 3 2 1

Library of Congress Cataloging in Publication Data

Holland, Isabelle.
  Abbie's God book.

  SUMMARY: A twelve-year-old girl expresses her
thoughts about God as she interacts with her family
and schoolmates.
    1. God—Juvenile literature. 2. Faith—
Juvenile literature. [1. God] I. McLaughlin,
James, 1948—   II. Title.
  BT107.H64   231'.044   81-21845
  ISBN 0-664-32688-9   AACR2

This is not a novel.
It is not a story with a plot.
This is a book of conversations—very
    personal conversations.
Anybody can start a God book.
You can, too.

I.H.

1

My name is Abigail Tyrrell. I am almost twelve. I have a twin brother, Andrew. We're not a bit alike. Last night I asked Father to tell me about God. Father said he didn't mind discussing God, but he'd like to find out what I thought. I told him I didn't think anything— much, which was why I wanted to ask him. But Father said I had to write down all the things I thought, and then we'd talk, which is just like him. Father is a writer, and he thinks everything should be written. But I sort of like to write, too. . . .

To begin at the beginning, as Mother would say, who is God?

When I was younger I thought he was somebody absolutely enormous who made everything. In fact, when I thought about Jesus, who is his Son, who also is God, which is very confusing, I imagined him sitting on a tremendous throne, like Lincoln in the Lincoln Memorial, and I'd see myself on top of his lap, which meant I was safe. And I would peek over the edge of his leg and see all the people below who were not safe and who were trying to get up to be safe.

Now I see that's pretty selfish, because all I felt was glad that I was okay, and as long as I said my prayers and didn't do bad things like lying, I'd stay safe. I didn't care about the others trying to haul themselves up on a thin string.

I told this to Miss Armitage, my English teacher at St. Hilda's School. She asked what would happen if I accidentally fell off.

"But—he's Jesus! He wouldn't let me fall off!" I said.

"Maybe you might fall off while he was reaching down to help someone climb up. Especially if you were getting in the way."

That upset me a lot. That night I added a special prayer asking God not to let me fall off.

2

Some of the kids at school say their parents don't believe there *is* a God.

"Well then, who made the world?" I asked one of them—Tony Bellows. He's in my class and is terrifically good at math.

"It's an accident," he said. "It just happened."

"I don't believe that," I said. "That's just silly." And I walked away. The rest of that day I kept telling myself off and on that it was silly. "Tony Bellows says the world is an accident," I said to my best friend, Sally Fraser.

"What kind of accident?"

"I mean—he says that God didn't make the world. It just happened."

Sally shrugged. "He's crazy. Or showing off. Are you going to the movie Saturday?"

"Mom says I can if I've finished my homework, and the movie's a G rating. But about Tony . . ."

"Oh, who cares about what Tony thinks! Can I read your essay for English class?"

It was funny, I thought, while she was looking over my essay. What Tony thought still bothered me. But it didn't bother her at all.

3

"Do you believe there is a God?" I asked Mother after school.

"Yes," Mother said. "Do you?"

"Yes, I think so."

"You sound doubtful."

"Well, what Tony Bellows said bothers me. He said the world wasn't made by God, because there isn't one; that it was a huge accident billions of years ago."

"Why does that bother you?"

The funny part was I really didn't know why it bothered me. "I don't know," I said.

"Well, when you know why it bothers you, and you want to talk about it, let's talk."

That night I had a bad dream. I dreamed I was falling off the lap of God into a black space When I woke up I turned on the light. Wadsy, my cat, was at the bottom of the bed. When I turned the light on he walked up and rubbed his head under my chin, purring loudly. I put my arms around him and hugged him, getting a lot of long tiger hair up my nose. But it was nice.

"You're God's cat," I said, and remembered then what Tony Bellows had said. Wadsy sat on top of me, purring, and when I finally turned off the light, he curled up on the pillow, still purring. Since he's huge, as well as inheriting long hair from some Persian ancestor, it didn't leave much pillow. But it was nice to have him there. I put my hand next to his back where I could feel him breathing and went to sleep.

The next day at breakfast I said to Mother, "Tony Bellows is wrong. It's not an accident. There *is* a God."

"I agree. But what convinced you?"

I thought about the warm, purring back sending out love. "Wadsy. He's not an accident. He couldn't be."

"True. There's something else that says God is."

"God is what?"

"God *is*. God is Isness."

I thought about that. "What else says so?"

"For one thing, the Bible."

"I hate Sunday School."

"I know you do. Why don't you come to church with us?"

"I hate church, too. I get bored."

12

Mother sighed. "Maybe that's one of the things that goes with being your age."

"Will it be different next year?"

"Who knows? We'll have to see when you get there." She grinned. "One year at a time! In the meantime, why don't you try reading the Bible —in small bits?"

"All right. When I feel like it."

The next day when I was not listening to the math teacher, I started thinking about Wadsy, and I found myself drawing in my math note-book a huge balloon which I marked "air." Then I drew a stick with legs which was me, my nose to the balloon, and another stick with four legs marked "Wadsy" with *his* nose glued to the bal-loon. There were Wadsy and I, both breathing in the air which went into Wadsy to make cat blood and muscle and bone and hair and into me to make human muscle and blood and bone and hair. But it was the same air, which meant . . .

"Abigail, what are you drawing there?"

"Oh, just a blimp."

"How about drawing twenty times forty-three instead?"

13

4

Wadsy turned up at our back door one morning when he was about three months old, yelling for food. I gave him some milk, and he's been my cat ever since. I named him Henry Wadsworth Longfellow because he was so small and because I was reading Hiawatha. He's now enormous, with a broad head, white front paws, a small snowflake on his nose, and the rest of him black and gray striped tiger. He's not the brightest cat in the world, but he's the sweetest and always sleeps with me.

Two mornings after my bad dream, Miss Armitage suggested in class that we keep a diary. I asked her afterwards if I could keep it about "Who is God?"

"All right," she said. "How are you going to begin?"

I didn't really know. "I'm not sure," I said.

"Well—I know about his lap, because you told me."

"Two nights ago I dreamed I fell off into a big black space."

"But here you are, so what pulled you out?"

"Wadsy." I told her about what Mother said about God being Isness.

"I am that I am," Miss Armitage said.

"What?"

"God said that, speaking to Moses out of the burning bush."

"Oh. I read about the bush. Did he mean Isness?"

"I think so. All past, all future, all everything is in God, and is now, going on."

"What about 1066 and 1492 and the Cave Man?"

"You'll get different answers from different people, but I think 1066 and 1492 and the Cave Man are all in Isness."

I collected my books and tied them up.

"You're going to be late to the next class," Miss Armitage said.

"Tony Bellows said there was no God—that it was all an accident."

"Well, then it's an accident with some pretty logical laws."

That made me feel better.

5

The diary didn't go too well. Miss Armitage
said, "Well, why don't you start with what God
isn't?"

"What *isn't* God?"

"What do you think he isn't?"

I was thinking about this off and on when I
went to art class.

"Don't use your eraser that way," Miss Briggs
said and took it out of my hand. By the time she
finished showing me how to use the eraser, the
page was gray and nobbly.

"And what's that?" she asked, pointing to a
small drawing in the lower corner of the page.

"It's a crocodile," I said. I like drawing crocodiles.

"What's that on its head?"

"A black hat."

"It doesn't look in the least like a crocodile,
and crocodiles don't wear hats." She picked up

the eraser again. In a few minutes the crocodile and his hat were also gray nobble.

"Daphne Benson over there has done a beautiful drawing of a kitten. Why don't you go over and look at it?"

I went over. There was an admiring circle around Daphne.

"That's a sappy-looking kitten," I said. "I have a cat, and he never looked like that, even when he was young."

"Abigail Tyrrell," Miss Briggs said, "you're jealous. That's a very ugly emotion."

"Why should I like her kitten?" I muttered. "You didn't like my crocodile."

"And don't mutter."

When I walked across the park on the way home I saw a sign: "Don't walk on the grass." Just because it said not to, I walked on it.

"Get off the grass. Can't you read the sign?" It was one of the park rangers, standing there, his hands on his hips.

"Don't step on the wet floor," Mother said when I got home, as I started to come into the kitchen.

At dinner Mother said, "Don't reach across the table, Abbie—ask Andrew to pass you the butter."

"Don't, don't, don't, don't," I said. "I bet one of the things God isn't is a lot of don'ts."

"What about the ten commandments," Andrew said. "We're studying them in Sunday School."

"Don't . . ." Mother started.

"*Do* have some ice cream," Father said. He passed the dish over to me.

It was like seeing the crocodile back on the page, complete with the black Spanish hat.

6

I started the diary the next morning. "If God isn't a tremendous person who made absolutely everything, then what is he?" I stared at the blank page for a long time.

"If you hurry, I'll drive you to school," Father called upstairs.

"How is your quest going?" he asked as we drove off.

"What's a quest?" Andrew asked. He was sitting in the back examining his new baseball.

"A search."

"A search for what?"

"For who God is."

"That's silly. Everybody knows who God is."

"All right, Andrew, who is he?"

"Well . . ."

"Yes," Father said, and winked at me. "Go on. Who is he?"

"Well, he made heaven and earth and all that

therein is. And Adam and Eve and Cain and Abel and Abraham and the Israelites and Joshua and David and the firmament and everybody."

"That doesn't mean he made me," I said. Somehow Andrew always had the answers, and I was getting tired of it. "And anyway, that's a long time ago and in another place and what does it have to do with me now? What is his Isness? Why are you smiling?" I asked Daddy.

"Because a great number of wise men in many lands down all the years since the beginning of everything have written thousands of books and preached millions of sermons trying to answer that."

"You see?" Andrew said. "What makes you think you have the answer?"

"I think she does," Father said. "And when she knows what it is, it will be the right answer for her."

"God doesn't speak to anybody anymore," Andrew said.

I looked at him in the rearview mirror.

"How do you know?"

"Yes, he does," Father said, drawing up outside the school.

"Who?" Andrew and I said together.

"Well—for instance, you. Me. But that's for another day. Now hurry or you'll be late for school."

7

I could hardly wait for Father to get home that evening. "How *does* God speak to you?" I asked as he was taking off his coat.

"Whoa, wait a minute!" Father said. "Let me catch my breath. My spirit isn't out of the traffic jam yet."

"But . . ."

"I said later, Abbie."

I felt pretty teed off. I'd been thinking about God speaking to Father all day (well, mostly all day when I wasn't thinking about something else), and now he couldn't talk to me. Maybe he'd been joking this morning. Maybe God hadn't spoken to him. Maybe he never spoke to anyone. Maybe Andrew was right. Maybe that part was all over and finished years and years ago and now you just read the Bible and went to church and didn't do a lot of don'ts and that was it.

"Why are you looking so grumpy?" Mother said, as I wandered into the kitchen.

"Because Father said this morning that God spoke to him, and I've been waiting all day to ask him how God speaks to him and now all he says is 'later.' "

"Well, it's hard to make the mental and emotional switch from office to home."

"You do it." Mother works mornings in a tree and plant nursery.

"I do a different kind of work. And anyway, I have an hour or so at home by myself before you get home."

"Do you think about God while you're working?"

"Always. It's sometimes easier there than here, when I'm handling green things and watching them and helping them to grow." She was putting soil into a small pot as she talked.

"What's that?" I asked.

"A sprig or so of pothos. I trimmed a big pothos today, and this is what I cut off."

I'd often seen Mother do this. People all around the neighborhood bring sick and dying plants so she can help them get well. A meow came from the door. Wadsy came into the room, tail up. Then he walked over, stared at my lap for a minute, and jumped up. I put my hand on his back. A deep purr started rumbling. I could hear it in my ears and feel it down my legs. There was a peaceful silence. The sunlight poured through the windows onto us.

"Wadsy is speaking to me," I said. "I can feel it in my legs."

Mother smiled and sprayed the leaves with water, touching them. "I can hear him. I think this plant is happy too."

"Do plants speak?"

"Yes."

"How?"

"I'm not sure. But if you know plants, you know how they feel." It sounded weird but I knew it was right. Plants that were brought to Mother looking limp and depressed would perk up and get green and shiny in a day or two.

The silence went on. I rubbed Wadsy gently under his chin. He rumbled. Mother put little stalks in a pot, held them, patted soil around them and then watered them.

Father burst into the kitchen. "Now," he said, "I'm ready to discuss God talking to me."

Mother looked at him over her half glasses and smiled. "Hush. You're interrupting him."

"Who?" Father said.

"God."

8

For about three weeks I didn't think about God at all. I was elected to the second basketball team and auditioned for a part in the Christmas pageant. Sally and I took up jogging, and Andrew brought a puppy home from the shelter.

"All right, Andrew," Mother said, looking down at the heap of black and white fur. "You can keep her, but only on condition that you raise her and you feed her. Understood?"

"Yes, okay. I promise."

"Cats are better," I said.

"They are *not*," Andrew yelled. "You wait and see. When she grows up, she'll chase old fatso Wadsy . . ."

"Don't you dare call Wadsy 'fatso'. . . . He's better-looking than that mangy . . ."

"I said QUIET!" Mother yelled.

When we both shut up out of sheer surprise (Mother never yells), she said, "No one is going to chase anyone. Your dog, Andrew, is only a puppy and will grow up loving Wadsy, and Wadsy will love the puppy, and if that isn't the case, they both go."

"What . . . ?" I cried, panicky.

"You heard me, Abbie. It's going to be The Peaceable Kingdom or else."

Andrew put the puppy down on the kitchen floor. She really was rather cute, with fuzzy black and white hair and a sharp nose. Waving a short tail, she made straight for Wadsy, who was lying on his cushion beside the oven. With a happy squeak, the puppy jumped on top of him. Wadsy went almost straight up into the air and then spat.

"You see . . . !" Andrew yelled.

"Be quiet, Andrew. Just everybody wait a minute."

For a long moment Wadsy and Puppy stood nose to nose, the puppy's tail going like an egg beater. Then the puppy licked Wadsy's nose, Wadsy blinked, backed, then very slowly started licking the puppy.

"You see?" Mother said. "The Peaceable Kingdom is in sight."

"What's the Peaceable Kingdom?" I asked.

"When the lion and the lamb will lie down together in safety."

"When's that going to happen?"

Mother sighed. "Not for a while yet—obviously. But when natural enemies like a dog and a cat are brought together when at least one is a baby, then it may work."

I leaned down and stroked Wadsy. "Where does it say about the lion and the lamb?"

"In the Bible."

I decided to look it up when there was no one around to bug me.

9

"Mom, do you think it makes any difference to God whether I kneel down or not when I say my prayers? After all, Buddhists don't."

"Buddhists don't what?"

"Don't kneel down."

"How do you know?"

"Jean Watkins at school is doing Zen meditation. She says they do the lotus position, which is sort of cross-legged, only more so."

Mother finished stacking the dishes. "No, I don't think it makes a difference to God whether or not you kneel." She got out a towel and started to dry her favorite coffee cups. "But it might to you."

"What do you mean?"

"Because I think your mind follows your body —not the other way around."

"I don't understand."

"If you slouch in a chair, say, I don't think it

has any effect on God. It doesn't make him feel sloppy. But it could make you feel sloppy, which could affect what you say to God and how you hear it back." She placed the cups and saucers on a top shelf, then turned around, smiling, and added, "However, that doesn't mean that when you're sitting down or walking along a street you can't pray."

"Why should I pray walking down the street?"

"Well, if you saw Wadsy, or any other cat, crossing the street in front of a car, mightn't you say a prayer that he not be run over?"

"Oh," I said. "Yes."

10

I was furious at Sally Fraser when sides were chosen for a round robin race jumping over the horse in the gym. She only chose me sixth.

"I thought we were best friends," I said afterwards, as we were putting back on our clothes.

"Of course you're my best friend," Sally said. "But you know you're no good at getting over the horse, and that slows everything down. And then the whole side gets mad."

"I don't say that to you when you want me to help you with your essays and spelling."

"That's different. Other people don't get mad at you because you help me."

"Sure they do. We get graded on the curve, and if I didn't help you, Ann and Dillon and Jane would get a higher grade. They'd be mad as anything if they knew."

"Are you going to tell them?"

"I don't know. I might."

"The next time we choose sides, I'll choose you first."

"That's bribery," I said and went home alone.

"What's the matter?" Mother said. I told her.

"You're right," she said. "It's bribery."

"I hate her," I said.

"That's an awful lot of negative emotion." She paused. "Every time you think about hating her, why don't you say a prayer for her?"

"For her? Why should I?"

"There are a lot of long theological reasons, but the best reason I can think of is—it'll make you feel better."

"It will *not.*"

"Try it."

"Please bless Sally and help her to see how wrong she is," I said the first night at prayer time. About the fourth night I heard myself say, "And help me to forgive her."

At this point I was beginning to notice how much I hated walking home alone.

Two days later our essays were handed back and Sally got a C.

"What's the matter, Sally?" the teacher asked. "This isn't up to your usual standard—and what happened to your spelling?"

Sally's cheeks were red. Then, when the red went, her nose went pink. I knew she wanted to cry. And I remembered suddenly that her father got mad when she didn't get good grades.

"How's the quest going?" Father asked me that night in the living room before dinner.

"I haven't been thinking about God lately," I said.

"What have you been thinking about?"

I told him about Sally and me.

"It's called forgiveness. And it has everything to do with God."

"I don't see why."

"What's the one prayer practically everybody says, and you say every night?"

"I don't see what the Lord's Prayer—oh," I said, after a minute. "You mean forgive us our trespasses?"

"Yes, that's exactly what I mean."

"That's hard."

"Nobody said it was easy."

"You mean I have to pretend it didn't happen?"

"You don't have to pretend anything." He rubbed his nose, which is a habit he has when he's thinking. "And you don't hide it, swallow it, brood over it, or blow it up out of all shape. You talk to her about it, remembering that she's not perfect, and neither are you." Father said after a minute, "Which would you rather? Sally as best friend or no Sally?"

I didn't say anything. If I said Sally, then I'd

have to stop being mad. If I said no Sally . . .

"Dinner's ready," Mother said, coming into the living room.

"Now I'll tell you about the monkey and the marble," Father said, as we got up to go into the dining room.

11

"What about the monkey?" I said, when we were all seated and served.

Father took a bite, then put down his fork. "There was a monkey who saw a brightly colored marble at the bottom of a glass vase with a long, thin neck. The vase was attached to a heavy brass pedestal and was too heavy for the monkey to move or turn over. So he put his skinny arm down, grasped the marble, and tried to bring it up out of the vase. He pulled and pulled, but it was no good. His hand around the marble was too thick to come up the vase's slender neck. So he dropped the marble and brought his hand out perfectly easily. But he didn't have the marble. So he put his hand down again, clutched the marble, and tried to bring it up. No go. At the end of a lot more trying he finally realized he could have his hand free of the vase, or he could have his hand *and* the

33

marble encased in the vase—not both."

There was a silence. Father and I looked at each other. Mother was watching us both. Then Father said, "You can enjoy your mad and your feeling of injury, or you can enjoy Sally as your best friend, not both. You have to choose."

The next day I saw Sally walking home very slowly. I walked a little faster. When I caught up I said, "You want me to help you with our history essay?"

"Yes. But it's no use saying you're good at jumping the horse, because you're not. But I'll pick you first at round robin anyway."

"That's not going to make me better at round robin, is it?"

"No. But it doesn't matter. I'll still pick you first."

"I thought forgiveness meant happily ever afterwards," I said to Mother that evening. "It doesn't."

"No, it means going on putting one foot in front of the other—no matter what."

12

Dillon Freemont asked me to go to church with him and his family one Sunday. He said they have a terrific preacher. I told him I didn't like church or Sunday School. He said once I heard their preacher, I'd love it. Mother and Father said okay, so I went.

When I got home, I wrote a new addition in my God book, in my list of "God Isn'ts":

"God isn't somebody who tells you you're lost for eternity when you say you don't like his preacher's sermon."

13

When I got home from school, Mother told me that Wadsy got hit by a car and was in the animal hospital.

"Why don't you say a prayer for him?" Mother said a while later. I was still crying, and she was holding me and rubbing my head.

That night I knelt down and asked God please to make Wadsy all right. Then I said the Lord's Prayer and Now I Lay Me Down To Sleep, and Blessed Jesus Meek and Mild, and Glory Be To The Father and every prayer I'd ever said or learned. Then I asked God again please to make Wadsy better.

The next day when I got home from school, Mother told me the vet said Wadsy was not getting along very well, that he was weak.

That night I said all the prayers I'd said before. Then I set my alarm for four o'clock so I would wake up and say them again the way somebody once said monks did. Then I said them again in the morning.

"What was that noise I heard in the night?" Andrew asked. His room is next to mine. I had turned off the alarm after the first ring but he must have heard.

"Yes," Mother said. "I thought I heard it too. Did you set the alarm for the wrong time, Abbie?"

"Mmmm . . ." I murmured and took a mouthful of cereal so I wouldn't have to answer. But I wasn't hungry.

That afternoon Mother put her arm around me and told me Wadsy was the same.

Before dinner I talked to a Catholic boy and a Jewish girl in my class and asked them to pray for Wadsy.

"What are you doing, Abbie?" Father asked.

I told him.

"All fronts covered, I see," he said. Then he said, "Abbie, do you think God listens to each religion with a different ear? That three prayers in three faiths are better than one?"

"Yes. And I've decided that I'll promise God I'll go to Sunday School if he'll just make Wadsy better."

"That would, indeed, be a sacrifice," Father said.

"I'll do anything."

37

"Honey, despite apparent examples to the contrary, I don't think you can bargain with God."

"I just want Wadsy to get better," I said, and burst into tears.

Father took me on his lap. "I have a suggestion. Why don't you tell God how you feel, ask him once more to make Wadsy well, and then say you'll turn everything—Wadsy and his recovery—over to him and you'll do your best to accept the results and thank him."

"What's the use of thanking him if Wadsy isn't well yet?"

"You can thank him for Wadsy's life and your having him all this time."

"I don't see that at all. Wadsy's dying, and I don't feel a bit like thanking God for anything."

"I thought you'd do anything."

That night I knelt down and said, "God, you know how I feel about Wadsy. He's the best cat in the world. You may have a lot of other cats under your care, but you can take my word for it. Please make him well." I paused. "Father says I have to turn the whole thing over to you. So here it is." I tried hard to say "Whatever you decide is okay." Maybe God heard it. It wasn't very loud. "And thanks," I muttered. Suddenly in my mind I saw Wadsy in his fat, furry splendor sleeping on my pillow. It was weird. But I could have sworn I heard his purr.

"Amen," I said and got into bed.

The phone rang at breakfast. "It's for you," Mother said.

I ran to the phone.

"Wadsy's much better," the vet said. "He's going to be okay now and can come home in a couple of days."

"Wowee! Terrific!" I yelled.

"Who was that?" Father asked.

I told him about Wadsy. "I guess it works," I said.

"Sure it does. But God isn't a machine. You don't put in a quarter and get out a candy bar, or put in the right prayer formula and get out what you want. You always have to know that sometimes the answer is 'No.' And that it's the best answer even though it sometimes takes years or even a couple of millennia to find that out."

"What's a millennia?"

"A long time. Hurry and I'll drive you to school."

14

The other day in class the teacher said the earth was billions of years old and humans and monkeys were descended from the same ape-like creatures.

Dillon put up his hand and said that wasn't true: the earth was made by God in six days and on the sixth day he made Adam and Eve, who weren't monkeys.

Tony Bellows said only stupid and uneducated people thought that, and the world was a cosmological accident.

Everybody started talking then.

The teacher let them talk while she started to clear the blackboard. Then she turned around.

"Tony, if you saw somebody who had been hit by a car and was lying on the side of the road, what would you do?"

"Call the police, I guess, or an ambulance."

"What if you were on your way to collect ten

thousand dollars which you wouldn't get if you were five minutes late? Would you stop? Or would you wait till you'd collected your money?"

Tony sucked on his pencil. "No, I'd go get the money first."

"Dillon, what about you? Would you stop?"

"Well . . . the Bible says—"

"I know what the Bible says," the teacher said, smiling. "Tony, why would you stop?"

"Well—it's right." He stopped, and then burst out, "If it was Rags who was hurt, I'd call the police first before I'd get the money."

"Who's Rags?" the teacher asked.

"My dog."

I decided Tony couldn't be all bad if he felt that way about his dog. "I bet you don't think Rags is a cosm . . . cosm . . . is an accident," I said.

"Sure I do. A terrific accident."

The teacher put down the blackboard eraser. "Just so long as you'd help somebody who needs it you can argue all you want about minor details like how the world started, and who's going to be saved."

"Minor details!" Tony almost exploded.

"Being saved is *not* a minor detail," Dillon said.

A girl who practically never said anything spoke up from the back of the class. "I think

41

everybody's going to be saved—sooner or later."

"What's the use of being saved if nobody's lost?" asked Dillon.

The teacher smiled. "You should talk to Abbie about God's lap and how not to fall off."

"God doesn't have a lap," Tony said.

"Are you positive?"

Tony opened his mouth, then closed it. The bell rang.

15

"God made Wadsy well," I said to Sally that day. "I prayed to him and he made Wadsy well. But Daddy says you have to be prepared for him to say no, because sometimes that's what he says."

"You always talk about God as he. Mother says God is she."

"That's nonsense. The Bible says God is he."

"I thought you hated the Bible."

"It's okay in spots," I said carelessly.

Actually, I wasn't hating it as much as I thought I would. When somebody isn't around telling me how holy the Bible is all the time, in a special reverent and gooey kind of voice (like a Sunday School teacher's I once had), it's not bad. In fact, they're some good spots in it. I especially like David and the story about the Prodigal Son, although I don't think being among the pigs is that bad. Pigs are nice. It was probably the horrible people who owned the pigs that the Prodigal Son didn't like.

"It's sexist," Sally said. "Why shouldn't God be a she?"

For some reason I found this almost as hard as the world being a cosmic accident.

"Mom," I said that night, "Sally's mother says that God is a she."

"Does it really matter?" Mom said. "Maybe God is both—or neither. Some churches call God Father-Mother."

That night I knelt down.

"Dear God, bless Mother and Father and Wadsy and Andrew . . ." and then my mind stuck on the picture of Christ in the Lincoln Memorial wearing a skirt. It upset me so much I stopped and got into bed and started to giggle. It was a very funny picture. The more I giggled, the more Wadsy purred.

The next morning I told Mother about it. She started to giggle, too. Then she said, "There are two things I'm going to say. One is, you can see why it's a mistake to visualize God."

"What's visualize?"

"Making a picture in your mind. Which is why the Jews and Mohammedans do not allow images of God or the prophets. You can't visualize

44

God. He-she-it is completely beyond anything we can imagine. The second thing is, if Christ, as in the Lincoln Memorial, had a skirt, you wouldn't be in such danger of falling off, would you?"

16

One day Miss Armitage didn't take her English class. There was a substitute teacher. She was middle-aged. She wore gold-rimmed glasses, and she was the fattest person I'd ever seen.

"Ms. Five by Five," Tony said under his voice when she was writing on the board.

"Five by seven, you mean," Dillon said.

Everybody around giggled.

The teacher turned around. "Now that's my name. I've put it up there so that you won't have any excuse for not knowing it."

On the board was "Miss Meagher," pronounced MEE-HER.

"Meagre," I said. People around giggled.

"Be quiet," the teacher said, sounding angry.

"Meagher by name and meagre by shape," Bart Hepburn, who was sitting behind me, sang quickly. I burst out laughing.

Miss Meagher turned bright red in the face. She walked down between the desks and stopped in front of me. When she walked, everything jiggled, which made me giggle more.

"What's your name?" she said.

"Abigail Tyrrell."

"All right, Abigail, you can go stand in front of the class in the corner there by the blackboard."

"That's for little kids," I said. "Nobody punishes us that way now."

"I do. Go stand there. This minute. Or I'll send you to the principal."

That made me furious, being punished as though I were a first-grader. "I'd rather go to the principal."

"All right, I'll take you there now."

Miss Meagher opened the classroom door, saw the monitor standing in the hall and asked her to come and stay in the class while she and I went to the principal's office. Out of the corner of my eye I could see everything jiggling as she walked. Somehow it wasn't as funny.

When we got there Miss Meagher told the principal that I preferred seeing him to standing in the corner.

"What happened?" he asked.

Miss Meagher said, "They were laughing and giggling. I told them to stop. Abigail here went on."

Then we all didn't say anything for a minute. It was strange, because I knew, and I was pretty sure the principal and Miss Meagher knew, what we were laughing at. But nobody spoke. Then Miss Meagher sighed. "I guess the reason's pretty obvious." Her eyes got pink.

"All right, Miss Meagher. I'll talk to Abbie."

When she'd gone, he said, "That's not very kind, is it?"

"I wasn't the only one who was laughing."

The principal, Mr. Miller, asked, "Has anybody ever embarrassed you in public?"

"Of course not," I said. And then I remembered. When I was in kindergarten I was sent to stand in the corner, and the teacher forgot about me. After a while I had to go to the bathroom and tried to attract her attention, but she wouldn't look and when I yelled she pretended she didn't hear. Finally I had an accident and everybody saw. Mother was furious and made her apologize to me. But it was still awful.

"Yes," I said. "When I was in kindergarten the teacher made me stand in a corner and wouldn't pay any attention when I had to go to the bathroom and I had an accident."

"Well—then you know how awful it can make you feel."

"But that wasn't my fault."

"But you think it's Miss Meagher's fault that she's overweight?"

"Well, everybody knows that if you're fat it's because you eat too much."

"No, everybody doesn't know it, not even the best medical experts. They say it depends on a lot of things—your genes, how your mother fed you, your metabolism, your body type, as well as the way you eat. But even if you were right—do you think it's kind? Would you like to be treated that way?"

Suddenly I remembered Andrew calling Wadsy fatso. And Wadsy didn't eat that much. "No."

"You know," Mr. Miller said, "when I was a boy I sometimes got teased for being Jewish."

"But that's not your—" I stopped.

"Fault? I don't think it's a fault at all. Besides, I like being Jewish."

There was another silence.

"Okay," Mr. Miller said. "You can go back to class."

Miss Meagher didn't say anything when I got back to class.

I saw her again while I was waiting for Sally to walk home. She came down the school steps —jiggling just the way she did before.

"Miss Meagher," I said suddenly.

She stopped. "Yes?"

"I'm sorry I laughed."

She smiled. She had a nice smile, which I hadn't noticed before. "That's all right."

I told mother that night about it, and asked her if she thought it ought to go into my God book.

"Of course. It's the Golden Rule."

"What's the Golden Rule?" I had a pretty deep prejudice against anything called a rule, whether golden or pink.

"Christ said, 'Do unto others as you would have them do unto you.' You don't like being embarrassed. So, don't embarrass other people."

"Oh."

17

"How's your God book going?" Daddy asked
that evening.

"Not too well. People have such funny ideas,
like Tony Bellows thinking God is an accident
and Sally's mother thinking she's a she. Even
though Mother says I wouldn't fall off his-her lap
if he was wearing a skirt, it makes me feel
funny."

"His-her lap? What are you talking about?"

I told him. Father laughed all the way through
dinner, breaking into chuckles every now and
then.

"It's not that funny," I said. I was beginning to
be annoyed. "And anyway, I don't believe God
talks to you."

"Why not?"

"You said you were going to tell me how God
talked to you and you never did."

"That just means I forgot or we were dis-

51

tracted. It doesn't mean he doesn't."

"All right, how?"

Father, who is passionate about fruit, started peeling an orange.

"When I was a conceited high school student and very full of myself, I went to church and heard a visiting Civil Rights activist-preacher who scolded us all for living in a white middle-class suburb—at least that was the way I took it. I told you I was full of myself and how wonderful I was, being president of everything at school—and here was this wild-eyed maniac trying to put us all down. I got so mad I walked out while he was talking and for three days that's all I could think about: who did this so and so think he was, yelling at us as if we hadn't collected money and clothes and petitions for the marches in the South? I was particularly furious, because I'd been chairman of the Inter-School Civil Rights support group. And we'd made a point taking odd jobs and giving up movies and sodas so we could donate the money to various activist leagues. My dignity and effort had been injured, and I'm sorry to say that for those three days I turned—mentally—into a combination Nazi and Klan member, and when anyone tried to talk sense to me I bit his or her head off.

"Then one day about a week later I went into the city to do some shopping. I grumped around in the rain buying this and that, collecting a lot of packages, which I stuck under my arms. Finally, on my way back to the station I saw some big navel oranges. You know how I feel about oranges—here, have a piece—" Daddy handed me a segment— "so I bought about eight of those. Then, outside the station, with hundreds of people around, the wet bag full of heavy oranges broke and they rolled all over the sidewalk. The trouble was, I was stuck. If I moved my arms, the rest of my packages, containing white shirts and underwear, would go all over the muddy pavement, and I could see my mother's face if I let that happen! So I was standing there, feeling stupid and helpless, with people walking past and around the oranges, when I heard a voice saying, 'May I help you?' And there was this old black woman. Feeling like a herd of idiots, I just stood while she picked up all those oranges. 'Now,' she said, 'what you need is a cloth shopping bag. I have one here.' And she took one from a pile of stuff under her arm, put the oranges in, and took the rest of my packages and put them on top. I tried to protest, but she went right on. Then she handed the bag to me. 'There, son,' she said. 'That's better,' and she walked off."

Daddy finished the last of his orange. "It doesn't sound like a great spiritual experience,

and it's hard to describe how I felt. But the near-
est thing I can think of is that it was like having
the poison drained out of an abcess. I got on the
train to come home, and I suddenly realized
that I wasn't angry anymore and didn't hate
anymore and that that was the miracle."

There was a silence. Daddy was a good story
teller. I could feel the way he felt when his bag
broke. "But what's that got to do with God
speaking to you?" I asked finally.

"Everything. I think God speaks to us through
people. We are his hands and feet and tongues.
He comes to us direct. But he also comes to us
through others."

"You mean, he was speaking to you through
that old woman?"

"Yes. The way he spoke through the Good
Samaritan."

"How do I know when it's God speaking to me
through somebody or not?"

"That's the hard part, but if it makes you feel
better about yourself or other people, it's usually
a good sign."

18

Daddy came in to say good night to me one night after I was in bed.

"Say your prayers?" he asked.

"No. I don't feel like saying them much anymore."

"Why not?"

"Well, I don't know who I'm talking to. As long as it was Christ in the Lincoln Memorial I was fine. I could see him easily. But now Sally says he's a she, and Jessica, a girl at school, says her mother says he's a being."

Daddy sat on the bed. "Do you miss saying them?"

"Yes." I hadn't thought about it before, but now that I did I knew it was true.

"Why?"

"Well, it was a lot of trouble, but I felt safe the other way."

"Don't you feel safe now?"

"Not in the same way."

"What are you afraid of?"

I suddenly remembered my dream of falling off God's lap into black space. And there was nothing there—no God, no Mother or Father or Sally or Wadsy or light. It was just a black hole. Suddenly I shivered. "Of the black hole."

Father said, "I have a suggestion. Why don't you ask God to help you solve this problem— that you want to pray to him but get blocked over who he is."

"But if I don't know who I'm praying to—"

"Just do it." He kissed me. "There's no black hole, and you're safe. But I want you to know it from the inside."

So before I turned out the light, I got out of bed and said, "Please, God, help me out of this so I can pray and be safe again."

That night I had another dream. I dreamed I'd fallen off God's lap into the black space and I was so scared I couldn't even scream. Then I looked around, and there below me was a huge golden net, and the strands on all sides went up, up, up to God's lap. The funny thing was, they came out of his hands and out of the hands of all the people up there, who were not going to let me fall.

"Oh," I said, and opened my eyes, and saw it was daylight. It occurred to me that the only reason I had thought it was dark—that the black hole was black—was because I had my eyes closed.

"Mom," I said at breakfast, "I don't think visualizing is such a bad thing."

"I didn't mean it was. Only that if somebody's mental image doesn't match yours, there's no point in getting into a state about it and deciding that one of you has to be wrong."

"So if Sally wants to think God is she, it's okay."

"Yes. But you hang on to your own ideas. One of these days you may find you think something else. But that's all right too. As long as you check out what you think."

"Who should I check it out with?"

"With God, with all the people and books you trust."

"Like—"

I knew she was going to say it, and she said it. "The Bible."

19

One day at school a week or so later we all heard that Tim Logan, a boy in my class I didn't much like, had died. He'd had some kind of kidney trouble and was often out of school. I felt vaguely guilty because I hadn't paid too much attention to his being sick, although we'd all signed get-well cards when he was in the hospital. He'd died suddenly.

"I guess he's in heaven," Dillon said.

"He's dead," Tony said. "His body decomposes and he becomes part of the earth. Worms eat him." He sounded pleased.

"Was he saved?" Betsy Hiller asked. She sat next to Dillon and went to his church.

The bell rang and we all went into the auditorium to see a film on the Kalahari desert in Africa.

When the camera first showed the desert all you could see was sand, miles and miles of it, no

shrub, no brush, no grass, not even a cactus—
nothing but sand.

I sat there, thinking about Tim, and how he
always knew how to needle you and how he
used to chase cats. And I also half listened and
watched as the film showed the insects and tiny
animals living in the sand, with the narrator
talking about them eating each other, and their
bodies going back into the sand. When it was
over, I felt terrible.

"What's the matter?" Mother said when I got
home.

I told her about Tim and what everybody said
and the movie about the desert. . . . After my
voice faded, Mother said, "So? What's worrying
you about that?"

"Well, it looks like Tony's right. You die and
your body just rots and gets eaten. If you're an
animal you get eaten before you rot. Everybody
talks about God being good. That doesn't look
very good to me."

"You're forgetting about the soul. The body
dies, but what people call your soul, or your
consciousness, lives. Even the Russians, who are
officially atheists, show pictures of plants whose
branches have just been cut off, but where those
same branches were still shows in outline—at
least for a while. In other words, we're more
than our bodies—or at least I think so. We have

souls or consciousness—whatever you want to call it."

"Dillon said Tim is in heaven. But how could he be in heaven if he was mean? And just because he's dead it's no use saying he wasn't mean, because he was. He threw stones at cats."

"Well then, wherever he is, he's learning that he and animals are closely related and not to throw stones at them."

"You mean you go on learning?"

"I think so."

I drank some milk and nibbled a cookie. "Then it's not all over when you die?"

"No."

"What about heaven and hell?"

"Heaven means being with God. Hell means choosing not to be with him. But you still have a choice, and many, many chances to choose."

Wadsy came and sat on my lap.

"Will Wadsy go to heaven?"

"Whatever made Wadsy himself—Wadsy in essence—came from God and will go back to him."

I poured some milk in a saucer for Wadsy and put it on the table. He jumped up and started lapping, purring loudly.

20

"Mom," I said one day. "Is there a devil?"

We were in the garden back of the house. Mother was transplanting some plants from pots to the flowerbed. I was chewing a grass blade and doodling in a notebook.

"I don't know. Some people say there is and some say there isn't. There's certainly evil in the world."

"Like what?"

"Unkindness, brutality, bigotry, indifference to other people's suffering, cheating, lying, killing—all the things we can do to destroy other people, or at least make them miserable."

"Does the devil cause that?"

"I've never been sure how much plain old human nature—wanting to have the most of everything, wanting our own way, wanting everything to be easy, wanting to be the best without effort—is responsible, and how much the actual power of evil is."

"Well, if God is more powerful than anything else, why does he let the devil do it?"

"Because he gave us free will to love him and choose his way, or not to love him and choose the wrong way. He won't force us. And he won't let the devil force us. We have to take the responsibility of choosing, and to know we choose."

"But what happens if you choose wrong and don't know it?"

"Then you will go on having choices until you know exactly what you're choosing and why. Look," Mom said, stacking the empty pots. "In everybody's life—even a murderer's—there have always been moments when he—or she—could have chosen to do something else. Maybe the first time he picked up a gun he could have chosen not to pick up a gun. Haven't there been times when you could have made, say, a bad choice, but didn't?"

I thought how it would be if Sally and I *hadn't* made up.

"Yes. So even if there is a devil, he can't do things to you unless you let him by choosing wrong?"

"No. But you can't choose right just on your own . . . well," Mom smiled, "not horsepower, but your own woman power. You have to ask for help. And God will always help when you ask him. Maybe not exactly the way you had in mind for him to help you. But he'll help."

"But I still have to do the choosing."

"Yes. But also remember that the man who chooses to pick up a gun is the result, not only of his own choices, but of other people's."

"How do you mean? How can I choose for somebody else?"

"I didn't say you choose for somebody else, I said the choices we all make affect not just us, but others. Suppose somebody made you angry. For about half a second you could choose whether to say something mean back or, instead, find out what's going on, what caused the anger. If you said or did something mean in return, then that person could go home in a bad temper and take it out there. And that particular buck gets passed all around, affecting the lives of a lot of people."

I thought of the golden net and all the hands holding it, and told Mother about my dream.

"Yes," she said. "Safety nets—as well as guns—are held by hands. You know," she said, sitting back on her knees, "I've often thought—the cross on which Christ was crucified was made of two pieces of wood, one horizontal and one vertical. It sometimes seemed to me that the vertical one served as a sort of lightning rod for all the unkindness, cruelty and wrong in the world. You remember in the history book you read where it said President Truman had a sign on his desk: 'The buck stops here.' Well the cross was Christ's sign saying, 'The anger, fear and revenge stop here.' He did not allow it to pass on but took it into himself. And it killed him."

"But it didn't stop. People can still be cruel."

"But we have a new method, a new weapon to use against it." She smiled. "A new net." Then she got up and came over to look over my shoulder to where I was doodling. "That's a crocodile."

"That's Kevin Crocodile," I said.

"Is that a hat he's wearing?"

"Yes."

"And what's that in his hand?"

"A net. Like a big butterfly net. In case one of his friends falls out of a tree or into a swamp."

21

"You know Kevin and his hat," Mom said about a week later. "The newspaper's running a competition for children's books by children up to fourteen. Why don't you make a book about Kevin and send it in?"

"The art teacher didn't like Kevin."

"That's just her taste. She could be wrong."

So for the next week or so I spent all my spare time—and some not so spare when I was in class —drawing Kevin and his adventures. Then I showed the drawings to Mother.

Mother grinned and laughed. "I like them," she said when she was through. "What they need are just a few captions." So I wrote one line of caption on each page. It was a story about Kevin Crocodile who saw a Spanish hat in a window and decided to buy it. He doesn't know it, but it's a magic hat. As he went through the day everybody commented on his hat. And whatever they said, he believed. If they said, "It makes you look fat," he felt fat. If they said, "It makes you look thin," he felt thin. If they said, "It makes you look handsome," he felt handsome. If they said, "It makes you look tired," he felt tired. Finally he threw the hat away.

"Is that how it ends?" Mother asked.

"Yes, that's the end."

"Well, send it in."

"Don't you like the end?"

"It's your book. You have to end it the way you want."

"How would you end it?"

"I'm not going to tell you. I would never have thought of Kevin Crocodile, so it wouldn't be right." Mother didn't move from that.

Daddy liked the book a lot. He took the pages to his office and had them photocopied there. Then he helped me staple and bind them and sent the book to the newspaper. The winners were to be announced in two weeks.

"Now we wait," Daddy said.

"Do you think I'll win?" I asked.

"I haven't any idea."

"Mom, do you think I'll win?"

"I don't know, darling. But even if you don't, I like Kevin."

"How's the God book going?" Daddy asked.

"I haven't had time for it lately."

22

The next week I had a huge fight with Andrew. This was when I discovered he'd sent in a book, too, but hadn't told anyone, not even Mother and Father.

"That's not fair," I said. "Everybody knows about mine."

"Course they do," he said in a rather superior way. "Because you told them."

"What did you write?" I asked.

"I'm not telling."

"Andrew knows about Kevin Crocodile but he won't tell me what he wrote," I said to Mother that day after school.

"He doesn't have to," Mother said. "Andrew's more of a private person than you are." She smiled. "He's not as much of a communicator. Besides—" She stopped.

"Besides what?" I had a curious feeling that I wasn't going to like what she said, and I didn't.

"He doesn't walk out on limbs as much as you do."

"What do you mean?"

"I mean if he doesn't win, not as many people know it. It's . . . it's probably less embarrassing for him."

It sounds crazy, but I hadn't thought about not winning. That night I prayed the magic prayer, telling God I wanted very much to win but letting the whole competition go after that —or at least trying to let it go—and turning over the results to him. I didn't tell anyone about my prayer. Every day I rushed home from school to see if there had been a letter or a phone call.

"They said they'd announce it in the paper," Mother said. "Abbie—I wish you wouldn't tie your whole happiness to whether or not you win. *You* liked Kevin. *I* liked Kevin. It would be nice if you won—but not that important."

"It's not really that important," I agreed, very casual. Somewhere a tiny voice inside me squeaked, Liar! "Truly," I said, and decided to be cool and not rush home anymore.

Two weeks later I tore home from school and went through the back door. Usually the afternoon paper is lying on the kitchen table, but it wasn't there this time. I went into the living room. Mother was at her desk.

"Where's the paper?" I asked.

68

"Here. Abbie—you didn't win, honey."

"Andrew?" It was my first thought.

She shook her head. "No. Some kid in a school across town." We looked at each other a minute. "What are you feeling right now—truthfully?"

I knew she was reading my mind. "Glad that Andrew didn't win," I said. I closed my eyes a minute. "Or anybody else in my school."

Mother got up and came over and put her arms around me. "It's called envy," she said. "We all have it to some degree. But it's not a very nice trait, is it?"

"No."

She sighed. "And it doesn't affect Kevin Crocodile. I liked him a lot."

"I think he's silly."

"Because other people decided Kevin's not number one, then you think he's no good. You're just like Kevin. He threw away his black hat—even though he liked it. And you're ready to discard Kevin."

"Well, if he was any good he'd have won." I felt furious and sick and disappointed and cross and didn't ever want to think about Kevin again.

23

Even though Andrew and I are twins we don't have much to do with one another. He plays with his friends and I play with mine. Once Mom said to me, "I wish you and Andrew were better friends." She looked at me. "Why do you think it is that you're not?"

I didn't have to think about it. "He's good at everything and he acts like he knows best and he thinks it's silly to say you're going to do something and not do it. And he's good-looking."

"In other words," Mother said, "he aggravates your inferiority complex, which you don't need to have anyway, because you're not inferior."

"He always gets As."

"You get As, too. When you bother to study."

"I get Cs, also."

"That's when you don't bother to study—things like math."

"It's boring."

"I wish you'd be nice to him."

"Why?"

"He needs to be loved."

"Why don't you tell him to love *me?*"

"How do you know I haven't?"

"Well, he's not doing it."

Mother sighed. "Never mind."

That wasn't what I wanted to hear either.

Mom and I were in the garden. She was weeding and I was helping her. That is, she was weeding and I was making noises with a grass blade.

"Did it ever occur to you that Andrew's drive to perfection is another way of asking to be liked? People admire Andrew, but they find it easier to love you. You're jealous of him but he's jealous of you. You have lots of friends—Sally, Debbie, Mona, Dan, Betty and Ann, just to start with a few. Andrew's popular in a general way. He's on a lot of teams. But he only has about two friends."

Pepper, Andrew's puppy, came slowly over and sat down. Wadsy, who was sitting on the other side, blinked, but didn't move. He had come to accept Pepper—more or less.

"I don't like the look of that puppy," Mom said. "She's thin and she's not eating."

"Why doesn't Andrew take her to the vet?"

"I've offered to drive him. But Andrew's been so busy he hasn't had time."

71

The puppy looked thinner and her fur seemed stringier. Suddenly, and as though she'd been listening, Pepper threw up. Mother stood up. "You're right. It's Andrew's dog and I wanted him to take the responsibility, but I can't let the poor little thing get any sicker."

I went with Mother in the car.

After the vet had examined her, he said, "You should have brought Pepper in sooner. In the first three months of their lives puppies and kittens die easily. She has a virus and high fever. You'll have to leave her here."

I was in the kitchen when Andrew came home from ball practice. Mother told him about Pepper. I don't know what I expected him to say or do, but I was surprised to see how white he went. His freckles stood out like mud spots.

"You should have taken her in sooner, Andy," Mother said. "I spoke to you about it Monday."

"Well, I was waiting for a time when I didn't have something I had to do."

"People—and pets—don't always wait around for the convenient moment."

"I didn't know she was that sick."

"That's because you weren't paying attention. If you have a pet, Andy, you can't just play with it from five-thirty to six and then forget about it when it's not on your schedule."

Andrew just looked at Mother and he went up to his room.

For the next two days Andrew called the vet twice a day. Pepper was still very sick. The third day the vet called while we were at school. Pepper had died. Mother told me when I came home, and then when she saw Andrew coming through the yard, told me to go upstairs. She wanted to tell Andrew alone. After a while, I heard the front door slam and saw Andrew streak up the block.

"He just looked at me and then ran off," Mom said. "He didn't say anything, but I knew he felt terrible."

Just before dinner I was passing Andrew's room. The door was open. On his bed was something I was sure was a copy of the book he had sent into the competition. The pages were stapled together and printed on the front were the words, "Pepper's Adventure." I went in and even though I knew I oughtn't to, I read it. There weren't any drawings, but the story was good—about how Andrew lost Pepper and looked for her in the town and then found her. It was sad, because you could tell from the book Andrew really liked Pepper.

"You have no right to be in my room, and you have no right to be reading my book."

Andrew was standing in the door. He came

over, snatched the book out of my hand and put it in a drawer.

"I'm sorry, Andrew, I'm really sorry about . . . about Pepper. Truly. And the book was good."

Andrew was standing by the desk, staring at the wall.

I went slowly over to him. Andrew didn't turn around. "It was my fault," he said, and started to cry.

I took his hand. Then I put my arms around him and kissed him. After a while he hugged me back, and we both cried.

24

The newspaper sent our books back.

"I still think Kevin shouldn't have thrown away his hat," Mom said. "Just because other people made comments about it."

I didn't say anything, but took it upstairs. Actually, I was going to throw it away. I was still mad at Kevin for not winning the prize for me. But I thought I'd take just one more look at him. When I got to the last page I stared at the drawing of Kevin's black hat lying on top of a heap of garbage on the town dump while Kevin, without his hat, is walking away. He looked naked and sad.

After a while I found myself doodling on a piece of paper. The doodle turned into another drawing: Kevin, leaving the garbage dump—his hat firmly on his head. Underneath was the caption, "This is my hat. I like it. It suits me. And I'm going to wear it."

For some reason I felt much better. People were always saying you shouldn't believe everything you read in the newspaper anyway.

That night when I said my prayers I said, "Please let Andrew be on your lap, too."

25

One morning about a week later Daddy said, as he was driving me to school, "How is the theological treatise coming?"

"The what?"

He grinned. "Your book about God."

"I haven't written in it much lately."

"I had a talk with Andrew a couple of days ago. He said you'd been a help to him when Pepper died."

"Andrew isn't so bad. I like him better than I used to."

"He said more or less the same about you." Daddy didn't say anything for a minute, then said, "You know, your God book isn't the only book in which you write your beliefs about God."

"What other book is there?"

"Your life. It's your biggest God book of all."

As we pulled up to school one morning Daddy said, "Do you still think of God as Lincoln in the Lincoln Memorial?"

"Yes."

"Did you ever see the Memorial?"

"Once when I was about six. I guess that's where I got the idea."

"Well—I have to be in Washington over the weekend, so I thought we'd all go. You can then see the Memorial again."

We left Wadsy with the vet at his house, and drove to Washington that Friday afternoon. Sunday we went to the Memorial and walked up inside.

I thought the statue would look smaller to me than it did when I was six. But it didn't. It looked much bigger. It was enormous. Lincoln's face was strong and gentle and sad. He must have been a terrific man, I thought. But I knew then that he was a man, a human, and I would never again think of God as like that statue.

We stood and looked at it for a long time, then walked down the steps. It was a beautiful day. The grass was a brilliant green and the Washington Monument across the Pool was glistening white. All the people around looked happy and friendly. I glanced at Andrew. He looked happier than he had since Pepper had died.

"Well," Daddy said. "Do you still think God is like that?"

"No. Lincoln's nice. But I now know God isn't like that."

I could see Mother smiling. It's hard to describe what I was feeling at that moment, except that it was wonderful and happy, as though I wanted that moment, when we were all standing on the green grass under the blue sky, never to end. Yet I couldn't wait for the next moment to come. I looked up at the sky. It almost seemed to ripple, like a great curtain, and everything—the people, a dog chasing a ball, the sky, the grass, the trees, even the building—appeared to breathe together, as though they were all alive with the same Life. I was tremendously happy and quite sure that God *Is*.

I took a breath, and then, suddenly, everything was ordinary again—nice, but ordinary. Andrew was scratching his nose and watching a softball game off to one side.

"Okay," Daddy said. "Let's go."

We began walking towards the car. I walked ahead with Daddy. "You know," I said, "about God. I just had the strangest, nicest feeling." And I tried to tell him about it—about the people, and the green, and the all-over happiness.

"That's wonderful," he said.

"It was terrific."

We walked in silence to the car. Then, as I opened the door, I looked back at the Memorial and the green breathing world.

"I think I'll start a new chapter in my God book," I said.

DATE DUE

JUN 0 8			
NOV 1 1 07			
DEC 18 1991			
FEB. 1 1 1993			
MAR 2 7 1993			
SEP 0 1 1994			
JAN 2 5 1996			
SEP 0 3 1998			
MAY 0 5 2001			
MAY 0 5 2001			